HIP-HOP

50 Cent

Ashanti

Beyoncé

Mary J. Blige

Chris Brown

Mariah Carey

Sean "Diddy"
Combs

Dr. Dre

Missy Elliott

Eminem

Hip-Hop:
A Short History

Jay-Z

Alicia Keys

LL Cool J

Ludacris

Nelly

Notorious B.I.G.

Queen Latifah

Reverend Run
(Run-D.M.C.)

Will Smith

Snoop Dogg

Tupac

Usher

Kanye West

Pharrell Williams

APR 2009

Beyoncé

Rosa Waters

Mason Crest Publishers

Beyoncé

FRONTIS Beyoncé Knowles has conquered the music world, first as part of Destiny's Child and now on her own.

PRODUCED BY 21ST CENTURY PUBLISHING AND COMMUNICATIONS, INC.

EDITORIAL BY HARDING HOUSE PUBLISHING SERVICES, INC.

MASON CREST PUBLISHERS INC.
370 Reed Road
Broomall, Pennsylvania 19008
(866)MCP-BOOK (toll free)
www.masoncrest.com

Printed in the U.S.A.

First Printing

9 8 7 6 5 4 3 2 1

Library of Congress Cataloging-in-Publication Data

Waters, Rosa.
    Beyoncé / by Rosa Waters.
        p. cm. — (Hip-hop)
    Includes index.
Hardback edition: ISBN-13: 978-1-4222-0112-1
Hardback edition: ISBN-10: 1-4222-0112-0
Paperback edition: ISBN-13: 978-1-4222-0178-7
    1. Knowles, Beyoncé—Juvenile literature. 2. Singers—United States—Biography—Juvenile literature. I. Title. II. Series.
ML3930.K66W42 2007
782.42164'092—dc22   2006006474

Publisher's notes:
- All quotations in this book come from original sources, and contain the spelling and grammatical inconsistencies of the original text.

- The Web sites mentioned in this book were active at the time of publication. The publisher is not responsible for Web sites that have changed their addresses or discontinued operation since the date of publication. The publisher will review and update the Web site addresses each time the book is reprinted.

CONELY BRANCH

Contents

Hip-Hop Timeline   6

1 Dream-Come-True   9

2 The Beginning   19

3 Destiny's Child   29

4 Going Solo   37

5 Getting Personal   47

Chronology   56

Accomplishments & Awards   58

Further Reading & Internet Resources   60

Glossary   61

Index   62

Picture Credits   64

About the Author   64

Hip-Hop Timeline

1974 Hip-hop pioneer Afrika Bambaataa organizes the Universal Zulu Nation.

1988 *Yo! MTV Raps* premieres on MTV.

1970s Hip-hop as a cultural movement begins in the Bronx, New York City.

1985 *Krush Groove*, a hip-hop film about Def Jam Recordings, is released featuring Run-D.M.C., Kurtis Blow, LL Cool J, and the Beastie Boys.

1970s DJ Kool Herc pioneers the use of breaks, isolations, and repeats using two turntables.

1979 The Sugarhill Gang's song "Rapper's Delight" is the first hip-hop single to go gold.

1986 Run-D.M.C. are the first rappers to appear on the cover of *Rolling Stone* magazine.

1970   **1980**   **1988**

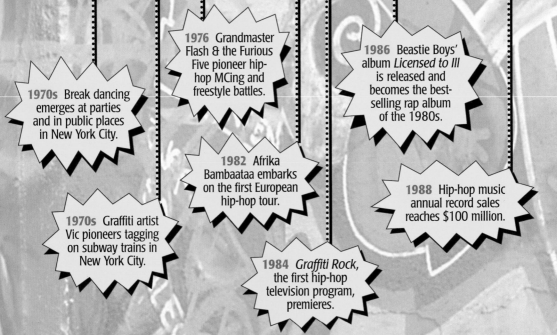

1976 Grandmaster Flash & the Furious Five pioneer hip-hop MCing and freestyle battles.

1986 Beastie Boys' album *Licensed to Ill* is released and becomes the best-selling rap album of the 1980s.

1970s Break dancing emerges at parties and in public places in New York City.

1982 Afrika Bambaataa embarks on the first European hip-hop tour.

1970s Graffiti artist Vic pioneers tagging on subway trains in New York City.

1988 Hip-hop music annual record sales reaches $100 million.

1984 *Graffiti Rock*, the first hip-hop television program, premieres.

1993 Rapper Snoop Dogg's album *Doggystyle* is the first debut album to hit the music charts at number one.

2006 Queen Latifah becomes the first hip-hop artist to receive a star on the Hollywood Walk of Fame.

1989 DJ Jazzy Jeff & The Fresh Prince become the first hip-hop artists to win a Grammy Award.

2003 Rapper Eminem becomes the first hip-hop artist to win an Academy Award.

2005 Hip-hop artist Kanye West appears on the cover of *Time* magazine.

1989 Rap is added as a new category to the *Billboard* charts.

1997 East Coast rapper Notorious B.I.G. (aka Biggie Smalls) is murdered.

2004 First National Hip-Hop Political Convention is held in Newark, New Jersey.

1989   2000   2006

1990s Hip-hop emerges in Europe.

1996 West Coast rapper Tupac Shakur is shot and killed.

2005 Rapper Will Smith opens the Philadelphia Live 8 concert as part of 10 simultaneous concerts held worldwide to bring attention to the extreme poverty in Africa.

1989 First gangsta rap album, *Straight Outta Compton*, is released by N.W.A.

2001 The hip-hop political action group, Hip-Hop Summit Action Network, is founded by Russell Simmons.

1992 Dr. Dre's album *The Chronic* is released; it redefines West Coast rap.

2006 The Smithsonian Institute National Museum of American History announces the creation of a new hip-hop exhibition scheduled to open in three to five years.

Five Grammy Awards, a clothing line with her mother, her own fragrance, and charity work: the year 2004 was an unforgettable one for Beyoncé, and just a clue of what was still to come for the young singer.

◄ 1 ►

Dream- Come-True

The 2004 Grammys opened with Prince and a young singer named Beyoncé singing a medley of his hits. Just a few minutes later, Beyoncé won the first televised award of the night for her contemporary **R&B** song "Dangerously in Love." Beyoncé thanked those she felt were most responsible for making her dreams come true—her parents and God.

Grammy Winner

Later in the night, Beyoncé stood in front of an elaborate framed **tableau** and sang her hit song "Dangerously in Love." At the end of the song, a dove landed on her outstretched hand.

By the next day, everyone was talking about Beyoncé. She had gone home with five awards that night, tying a record set by Alicia Keys, Norah Jones, and Lauryn Hill for the most Grammys won by a female artist.

A show-stopping performance with music legend Prince at the 2004 Grammy Awards brought Beyoncé praise from the critics and admiration from fans, both new and old. She capped off the evening by winning a record-tying five awards.

Living the Dream

The year that followed the Grammys was a busy one for Beyoncé. In March, she went on tour with Alicia Keys and Missy Elliott for the Verizon Ladies First Tour (promoted by Clear Channel Entertainment). The months after the tour were packed with awards and appearances for Beyoncé.

InStyle

YOUR OWN PERSONAL STYL

August £3.10

Love your legs!

Easy steps to beach-perfect pins

Kate Moss
Secrets of a style icon

Sexy
in the city
How to wear fashion at work – without frightening your boss

Beyoncé
'I have curves – most women do – and I'm happy with them'

40 hot sunglasses

Voted **Magazine of the Year 2004**

You're beautiful, baby
The most flattering pregnancy wardrobe

Beyoncé is also famous for her sense of style; she loves fashion! In 2004, she and her mother, Tina, announced the creation of House of Dereon, their new clothing line, named after Tina's mother and Beyoncé's grandmother.

She was on television numerous times, including *Soul Train*, *Girls on the Top*, *The Wayne Brady Show*, and multiple appearances on *On Air with Ryan Seacrest*. She won the British award for Best International Artist, the MTV Video Music Award for "Naughty Girl," the BET award for Best Female R&B Artist and Best Collaboration (for her song "Dangerously in Love"), the Radio Music Award for Artist of the Year, the People's Choice Award for Favorite Female Performer, TRL's First Lady Award, the Soul Train Music Award for Best Female R&B/Soul Album (for *Dangerously in Love*), the Sammy Davis Jr. Award for Female Entertainer of the Year, and the NAACP (National Association for the Advancement of Colored People) award for Entertainer of the Year.

A Sense of Style

In September of 2004, Beyoncé found time to announce that she and her mother were opening a new clothing line together, the House of Dereon. The line was named after Beyoncé's grandmother (Tina Knowles' mother), honoring the woman who worked as a seamstress for a living and imparted a love of fashion to her daughter. According to Newswire, "Agnes Dereon serves as both the inspiration and mentor for Beyoncé and Tina Knowles. Her artistic spirit **inaugurated** three generations of stylish women and continues to inspire today."

Beyoncé added:

"To me, this is the greatest way to enter into the fashion world. Inspired by my grandmother, working with my mother and pursuing a dream we have all had for many years. . . . "

Reaching Out to Others

Beyoncé took on another project in 2004 as well: she contributed to the Texas Music Project's CD (along with other artists, including Clint Black, Eric Clapton, George Strait, and Bonnie Raitt). The CD was dedicated to raising awareness and funding for music education in Texas schools. Proceeds from the CD's sales benefited Texas schools through grants for music education. The Texas Music Project was grateful for Beyoncé's and the other artists' contributions. The project's president, Bruce Orr, explained to Newswire why the funds were needed so desperately:

Giving back is important to Beyoncé, and she participates in many charity events. Here she is shown performing in 2004 at the 16th Carousel of Hope Ball, a fund-raising event for the Barbara Davis Center for Childhood Diabetes.

"Music teachers from across the state tell us programs are being eliminated and they are in desperate need of funds. . . . And these teachers are not just concerned about the next generation of musicians. They see how music touches all students, building self-esteem, teamwork and strengthening families and communities, while reducing drop-out rates."

Beyoncé knew firsthand the effect music can have on a child's life. Throughout her life, music had been central to her self-esteem—and music had been the fabric that held her family together as well.

Beyoncé found time in 2004 for another charity event. In October, she joined Faith Hill and Josh Groban at the Carousel of Hope, a gala event in Beverly Hills, California, that raised funds to benefit childhood diabetes. The star-studded event included other big names as well: Oprah, Jay Leno, and Halle Berry, and many others were there.

A Busy Year

In October 2004, Beyoncé launched her own fragrance, True Star. She also took part in many advertising campaigns for big-name companies like Pepsi, L'Oreal, Tommy Hilfiger, and McDonalds. By November, she was on tour again, this time with her group, Destiny's Child.

When an interviewer from London's *Independent* spoke with them, the young women were exhausted. Beyoncé told the interviewer:

"We've always worked well under pressure, but there is no way we will ever put ourselves through something like this again. It's just not worth all the pressure, all the stress. . . . My whole life right now feels like an endless round of promotion."

Kelly Rowland, another member of Destiny's Child, added, "We're not complaining, because we love making music, we really do."

Shining Destiny

Beyoncé kept up the same busy pace in 2005. She toured Europe again with Destiny's Child, and then came back to the United States in July to finish the tour at home. The Destiny Fulfilled . . . and Lovin' It Tour was built around state-of-the-art concerts. The sets,

Big-name companies like L'Oreal, Tommy Hilfiger, Pepsi, and McDonald's were just some of the corporations that recognized—and took advantage of—Beyoncé's power as a celebrity spokesperson in 2004. Here Beyoncé practices a high kick for a Pepsi commercial.

lighting, and staging were spectacular—and of course the costumes were designed by Beyoncé's mother and the House of Dereon. Singer Amerie, **platinum** recording artist Mario, and emerging urban artist Tyra toured with the group.

Beyoncé's group had a good year. They received the 2005 BET award for Best Group, and the American Music Awards for Favorite Band, Duo or Group and R&B Favorite Album. Destiny's Child was also given four Grammy nominations: Best R&B Performance by a

Duo or Group with Vocals (for "Cater 2 U"), Best R&B Song (also for "Cater 2 U"), Best R&B Album (for *Destiny Fulfilled*), Best Rap/Sung Collaboration (for "Soldier," performed with T.I. and Lil Wayne). Beyoncé had two nominations of her own, one for Best Female R&B Vocal Performance (for "Wishing on a Star") and the other for Best R&B Performance by a Duo or Group with Vocals (for "So Amazing" with Stevie Wonder). During the holiday season, Destiny's Child was also seen on televisions across America, when they were featured in WalMart's Christmas ads. Mattel even released Destiny's Child Barbie dolls in time for the holidays!

In 2005, Destiny's Child (shown here, left to right, Kelly Rowland, Beyoncé Knowles, and Michelle Williams) went back on tour with the Destiny Fulfilled . . . and Lovin' It Tour. The show featured state-of-the-art sets, lighting, and costumes by House of Dereon.

Tribute to a Friend

In the spring of 2003, Beyoncé and Luther Vandross remade a duet called "The Closer I Get to You," which had originally been performed by Roberta Flack and Donny Hathaway. In Beyoncé and Luther's version, they flipped the vocal parts, and Beyoncé sang Donny Hathaway's original part, while Luther sang Roberta Flack's. Luther included the song on his album titled *Dance with My Father*, and Beyoncé used it on her upcoming album as well.

When Beyoncé got her 2004 Grammys, Luther Vandross had also been a winner. Vandross, who had suffered a debilitating stroke in 2003, won four awards, including song of the year for co-writing "Dance With My Father" with Richard Marx. (He also won best male R&B vocal performance for the song and best R&B album for the album of the same name.) Beyoncé and Vandross won an award together as well, for their duet.

A year later, in 2005, Vandross died, and the music industry lost one of its leading lights. Beyoncé did what she could to help the world remember the man who had shared her glory at the 2004 Grammys. With Stevie Wonder, she sang "So Amazing," on a Vandross tribute album by the same name.

Keeping Up the Pace

Beyoncé never seemed to stop. She starred in the *Pink Panther* (released in February 2006), and released the movie's theme song as a single ("Check On It"). She was featured on Pharrell Williams's solo debut album, also released in February 2006. With one movie out, she began work on another, *Dreamgirls*. Once that was out of the way, in the spring of 2006, she got to work on her second solo album.

Beyoncé's life was truly a dream-come-true. By the time she was twenty-five, she had come so far, so fast.

Beyoncé credits her parents, Tina and Mathew, for much of the success she and Destiny's Child have received. Her family's support has been very important to her. Here, she and her parents are seen attending the MTV Movie Awards in 2003.

2

The Beginning

In 1981, in Houston, Texas, a young couple named Tina and Mathew Knowles were expecting a baby. They had an agreement: when their baby was born, Tina would pick the first name, and Mathew would choose the middle name. On September 4, they had a little girl—and they named her Beyoncé Giselle Knowles. Beyoncé—which rhymes with "fiancé"—was Tina's maiden name, and she thought it made a beautiful first name for her little daughter.

Tina owned a hair salon, and Mathew was a medical equipment salesman. In the 1960s and '70s, Mathew had marched in **civil rights demonstrations**. He believed in standing up for what was right, and he had done his part to help bring equal opportunities to African Americans. Now, in the '80s, he was prepared to use that same determination on behalf of his family. The family wasn't rich, but as the years went by, both Beyoncé's parents worked hard to make sure she and her younger sister Solange had everything they needed to be happy. Both sisters attended private schools, and they lived in a nice home.

When Mathew and Tina Knowles were in high school, they had sung in their school chorus and participated in talent shows. They never had the chance to go on professionally with their singing, but they made sure that their girls grew up with an appreciation for music. A favorite family activity was to gather around the piano; Mathew played, and Tina and the two girls sang along.

As a little girl, Beyoncé loved to sing. By the time she was in the first grade, she had made up her mind about what she wanted to do when she grew up: she wanted to be a professional singer. Her parents were impressed with their daughter's talent, and they did all they could to encourage her.

When Beyoncé sang, she turned into someone else, someone confident and sure of her own ability. As an adult, she told CNN's Headline News:

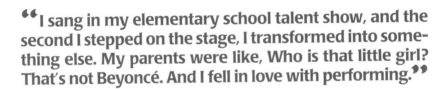

"I sang in my elementary school talent show, and the second I stepped on the stage, I transformed into something else. My parents were like, Who is that little girl? That's not Beyoncé. And I fell in love with performing."

The song she sang at her first talent show was John Lennon's "Imagine." When Mathew heard his daughter's voice soaring out over the school auditorium, he was so excited that he decided to help his daughter form a singing group with five other girls. They called the group Girls Tyme.

The little girls sang together as often as they could. They practiced and improved their performances. Whenever they could, they signed up for talent shows. With each new experience, they gained confidence.

Disappointment

By the time Beyoncé was eleven years old, she and her father were both convinced she was ready for fame and fortune. So they were excited when they learned that Girls Tyme was going to appear on *Star Search* on national television. Beyoncé knew she and her friends sounded good together.

Like *American Idol*, *Star Search* gave young people from across America the chance to perform and show off their talent in front of a panel of judges. The winner of each week's show would go on to compete for a grand prize. Christina Aguilera and Britney Spears, as well as other famous performers, had gotten their start on *Star Search*. Beyoncé was convinced this was just the opportunity she had been waiting for.

When the big day finally arrived, the six girls went together to the television studio. They waited their turn nervously, joking with each

Tina Knowles owned a hair salon when Bèyoncé was a child. Beyoncé worked in her mom's salon, even singing to the customers. Here, Beyoncé and her mother share their love of fashion, attending the CFDA Fashion Awards in 2004.

Mathew Knowles has been a driving force in Beyoncé's career. The salesman quit his job to manage his daughter's and Destiny's Child's careers. In 2004, he and Beyoncé attended the 46th Annual Grammy Awards, where his dedication was rewarded with Beyoncé's five awards.

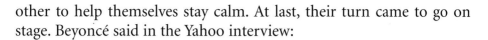

other to help themselves stay calm. At last, their turn came to go on stage. Beyoncé said in the Yahoo interview:

> **"The song we did was not good; we did the wrong song. When they said they gave us three stars, we were forcing a smile because we lost. We couldn't even last until we got backstage; the tears were already falling. We were devastated; we thought our lives were over. It definitely humbles you."**

After the disappointment they had had on Star Search, not all the girls in the group wanted to keep going. The group disbanded, but Beyoncé's father helped her form a new group of four girls. As always, Mathew Knowles was right behind his daughter, making sure she had whatever she needed to grow creatively.

A Father's Dedication

Mathew Knowles believed so much in his daughter's talent and her drive to succeed as a singer that he took an enormous leap of faith: he quit his job as a salesman and became the girls' full-time manager. Years later, Beyoncé told *Ebony* magazine:

> **"My father . . . would always book shows for us. We would try to perform once a week, and in the summer, twice a week. I'm very lucky. Both my parents support me and my career."**

Mathew and Tina had faith in their daughter's talent—but when Mathew quit his job, it meant the family had a lot less money. In order to make ends meet, Beyoncé's parents sold their home and their cars. The family moved into an apartment. While her father managed the group, her mother made their costumes and styled their hair.

Over the next few years, the girls performed under a variety of names—Something Fresh, Cliché, The Dolls—and finally, Destiny's Child. While Beyoncé and the other girls rehearsed over and over, week after week, Mathew and Tina Knowles offered their advice. And while the girls sang and sang and sang, Tina did her best to support her family by making her hair salon a success. Some of the girls' best feedback came from Tina's customers. Beyoncé said in an interview for BeatBoxBetty.com:

"We'd . . . go to my mom's salon, Headliners, to test out our new songs on all of her customers. We'd get tips too! My best memories are in that salon—sweeping up hair and trying to be all grown up on the phone like I was a receptionist."

Growing Pains

Everyone who performs feels nervous sometimes, and Beyoncé was no exception. After all, she was still just a little girl—and most of the time, she was quiet and shy. But Beyoncé learned a trick for dealing with her nervousness. Whenever she felt stage fright, she simply pretended to be someone else, an imaginary girl named Sasha who was never afraid. Beyoncé might have been shy but Sasha was outgoing and confident.

Beyoncé's imagination helped her become the person she wanted to be on stage. Eventually, she felt almost more at home on stage than she did anywhere else. In an interview with *Film Monthly*, she said: "I felt that I could express myself and perform and do what was in my heart on the stage. I felt comfortable on the stage."

But Beyoncé was a lot less comfortable when she was at school. She wore braces and glasses, she was a little chubby, and she was afraid to speak out loud in her classes. In the interviews she gave when she became an adult, she said she was unpopular and a "geek." In the group's autobiography, *Soul Survivors: The Official Autobiography of Destiny's Child*, she wrote:

"No one would have believed that my mom owned her own beauty salon, because I went out of my way not to look too pretty. I did everything I could not to draw attention to myself."

When she was at school, Beyoncé kept her singing a secret. She didn't want people to think she was showing off, and she was embarrassed to talk about her performances. In the group's autobiography, she wrote:

"People thought I was stuck-up . . . because I was quiet. Some people misunderstand quietness and shyness; they think you're full of yourself. They don't even give you a chance. With those two strikes against me already, there was no way I was going to let anyone in school know I could sing! That would just make things worse. **"**

As Beyoncé grew older, she continued to struggle with her self-image. She must have felt almost as though she were two different people. Sometimes she was a quiet, shy schoolgirl—and other times, she was a confident, talented performer. Every day, she endured the hours at school. Then she would come home and turn into her other self, rehearsing for

Beyoncé's adolescence was filled with many of the same insecurities felt by most teens. She was very shy, she wore braces and glasses, she was chubby. But Beyoncé worked through those growing pains to become a successful and happy singer, actress, and person.

as long as eight hours every night. It wouldn't have been surprising if sometimes she wondered who was the real Beyoncé. But as busy as her life was, she didn't have much time for thinking about it.

Relationships That Made the Difference

Beyoncé's father wanted so badly for his daughter to be a success that he pushed her forward in whatever way he could. He decided her

Beyoncé has always been close to her sister Solange. When group member Kelly Rowland moved in with the Knowles family, Beyoncé felt like she had two sisters. Here, Beyoncé (left) and Kelly (right) attend the opening of Solange's (center) film *Johnson Family Vacation* in 2004.

performances would be more polished and professional if she changed the way she looked, so he put his daughter on a health and exercise program. Now, before school every day, she had to go for a three-mile run. Her new diet consisted of mostly soup and skinless chicken breasts.

Mathew Knowles may have pushed his daughter hard, but he was only doing everything he could to help her achieve her dreams. He cared about the other girls in Destiny's Child as well. When he discovered that Kelly Rowland's single mother was having a hard time financially, he and Tina suggested that Kelly come to live with them.

Kelly was grateful for their help, but she was also grateful for all her mother had done to help her. She told *Ebony* magazine:

> **"I think my mom is a really strong person, and I'm just blessed to have three parents in my life. Tina and Mathew have been like my mother and father."**

Already close to her little sister, Solange, Beyoncé loved having a new sister, and Kelly felt the same way. She told *Ebony*:

> **"Our relationship goes deeper than Destiny's Child. That's my sister, and I love her and I know she feels the same way about me. We have each other's back, no matter what."**

Through all the professional ups and downs that lay ahead, the two girls' friendship endured. It was a constant in their lives, something that helped to make them strong through all the challenges that lay ahead.

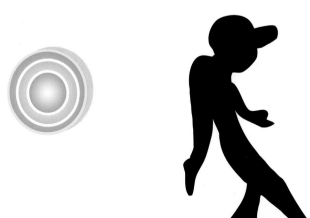

With a record contract, a song for a hit film, and tours with TLC and Christina Aguilera, 1997 was a big year for Destiny's Child. Shown here in a photo from 1998 are (clockwise from bottom left) Kelly Rowland, LeToya Luckett, Beyoncé, and LaTavia Roberson.

3

Destiny's Child

Mathew Knowles' dedication and the four girls' talent finally shot Destiny's Child into the limelight, where they drew the attention of the music world. Success was on its way, just as Mathew had always known it would be. He had pushed the girls hard, but now his efforts were paying off.

Columbia Records Makes a Deal

In 1997, Destiny's Child signed a contract with Columbia Records. The group's first big opportunity came with a song called "Killing Time" for *Men in Black*, the movie starring Will Smith and Tommy Lee Jones. The group also toured as the opening acts for TLC and Christina Aguilera.

Soon after that, Beyoncé and the rest of Destiny's Child moved to Los Angeles, where they got to work on their first album. *Wyclef Jean and Jermaine Dupri produced Destiny's Child.*

This was an exciting time for Beyoncé, but her life wasn't always easy. While other girls her age had nothing to worry about but dates and grades,

Beyoncé had grown-up responsibilities. Instead of going to high school, where she would have laughed and talked with other kids her age, she had a tutor, "which is very serious and boring," she told *Film Monthly*, "nor was I ever a cheerleader or went to games or any of those things."

In 1998, when Beyoncé was sixteen, the group released their first single from the album, "No, No, No." Beyoncé never forgot the first time she heard one of her songs on the radio.

She and her parents had just driven to pick up Beyoncé's sister, Solange, from school, Beyoncé told *Launch*. As Solange and her friends walked toward the car, the song started playing.

"It was unbelievable. We jumped out and started running around the car. We screamed and laughed and cried and danced and sang and all of that. My sister was so embarrassed. And then she heard the song, and she's like, 'Aaaahhh!' And she dropped her bag and started running around the car too."

Happy Birthday, Whitney!

A few months later, Beyoncé had an even bigger thrill: Whitney Houston invited Destiny's Child to her birthday party in New York City. Beyoncé told *Launch*:

"We got some money and put our happy butts on the plane and went straight to the party. We even dressed alike, like we were going to perform. And Whitney came and hugged us, and she said that she loved us. We were just in awe."

Lady of Soul

The year 1998 was a good one for Destiny's Child. The group won three awards at the Soul Train Lady of Soul Awards.

Destiny Child's first album was a success, and they went to work on their next one, *The Writing's on the Wall*, which was released in 1999. The album featured two number-one hits, "Bills, Bills, Bills" and "Say My Name." "Bug-A-Boo" and "Jumpin' Jumpin'" were also popular songs,

One of Destiny's Child's biggest thrills was when superstar Whitney Houston (shown here in 2004) invited them to her birthday party. There the young women learned that Whitney was a big fan of the group.

and "Say My Name" won two awards at the 2001 Grammys for Best R&B Performance by a Duo or Group with Vocal, and Best R&B Song.

Beyoncé wrote many of Destiny's Child's songs herself. In them, she had the chance to express herself, including some of her frustrations. Being a star was hard, she had discovered, and on top of everything else, the pressure to be physically perfect was a heavy burden to bear. Her song "Bootylicious" spoke out on behalf of a woman's natural looks. Internet Movie Database reported that she said:

"I wrote that because, at the time, I'd gained some weight and the pressure that people put you under,

the pressure to be thin, is unbelievable. I was just 18 and you shouldn't be thinking about that. You should be thinking about building up your character and having fun and the song was telling everybody just forget what people are saying. . . . It's a celebration of . . . women's bodies. **"**

Turning frustration and rebellion into music worked well for Beyoncé and Destiny's Child. But just when everything was going so well, things came to a shuddering halt.

The Lawsuit

Beyoncé was horrified when her friends LaTavia Roberson and LeToya Luckett quit the group in 2000. Shortly after, they filed a lawsuit against Beyoncé's father. LaTavia and LeToya accused Mathew of mismanaging Destiny's Child's money. They also said that he showed **favoritism**, promoting his daughter as the group's star, rather than working on behalf of all the girls equally.

For Beyoncé, Destiny's Child had been like another family. When two members walked away in anger, she was almost as hurt as if her parents had suddenly told her they were abandoning her. Beyoncé sunk deep into depression, retreating from the world as she once had when she was in school. For a month, she barely left her room.

Whatever Mathew Knowles thought about the lawsuit, he was too dedicated to Beyoncé's success to let the tension get in his way. He immediately hired two new singers, Michelle Williams and Farrah Franklin, to replace LaTavia and LeToya.

When it came time to create the video that went along with "Say My Name," a single that had already been released from Destiny's Child's second album, Michelle and Farrah lip-synched to the voices of LaTavia and LeToya. Beyoncé was learning a painful lesson about the entertainment business: the show always goes on, no matter the personal upsets.

But she was upset all over again five months later when Farrah announced that she too wanted to quit the group. Farrah wasn't used to the long hours of rehearsal that Mathew demanded of the group. She was a teenage girl, after all, and she was tired. She wanted to have a life.

This time, instead of hiring another replacement, Mathew decided to stick with what he had. Destiny's Child became a trio instead of a quartet.

Meanwhile, LeToya and LaTavia's lawsuit settled out of court, but rumors were still circulating about Destiny's Child. Beyoncé, who had always hated the wrong kind of attention, was miserable, especially when she heard that people were blaming her for the group's breakup.

But this time, Beyoncé did not retreat to her room. She went back to work and did what she could to build a positive atmosphere. She told *Launch*:

Michelle Williams and Farrah Franklin replaced LaTavia Roberson and LeToya Luckett when they left Destiny's Child in 2000. After Farrah left, the group became a trio, which they have remained. In this photo (left to right), Beyoncé, Michelle, and Kelly are shown recording a track.

"I can sit here all day and say I'm not a **diva**, but it won't matter, because people just have to be around us and see how we support each other. That's how a group is supposed to be."

Survivor

Beyoncé proved she had what it took to keep going; she was a survivor. She wrote and produced much of Destiny's Child's next album, which was named—appropriately—*Survivor*.

In 2001, Destiny's Child's album *Survivor* hit the charts in the number-one spot, and sold more than nine million copies worldwide! The group won two Grammys and many other awards. Beyoncé became the first African American woman to win Songwriter of the Year from ASCAP.

The album included the hit single "Independent Woman Part 1," from the *Charlie's Angels'* movie soundtrack. In 2001, the album **debuted** at number one on the *Billboard* list, and it went on to sell more than nine million copies around the world. The album's success not only proved that Destiny's Child was still as strong as ever; it also proved that Beyoncé was as talented a songwriter as she was a singer.

Later in 2001, Destiny's Child won Grammy awards for Best R&B Song and Best R&B Performance by a Duo or Group for "Say My Name." The group also won five *Billboard* awards, including Artist of the Year. Beyoncé won several awards in her own right as well, including the Songwriter of the Year Award from the American Society of Composers, Authors, and Publishers Pop Music Awards. She was only the second woman to ever win the award, and the first African American woman.

The year 2001 was a turning point for Destiny's Child. After the success of *Survivor*, Beyoncé, Kelly, and Michelle were each offered the chance to do solo albums. They talked it over and decided to take a break from Destiny's Child. Beyoncé and Kelly had been singing together for most of their lives, but now the time was right for them to try some things on their own.

Despite their success, Destiny's Child decided to take a break from performing together, and Beyoncé used it as an opportunity to spread her wings. She performed and recorded as a solo act, and she began an acting career.

4

Going Solo

Time away from Destiny's Child gave Beyoncé the chance to pursue new options—including acting. She had never had any acting training, but this was something she wanted to do. She believed in herself, and so did her family. So she went to some auditions and waited to see what happened.

A New Chapter

Beyoncé's first role was in an MTV movie that was based on the opera *Carmen*. After that, she landed a starring role in the 2002 movie, *Austin Powers in Goldmember*; she played Foxxy Cleopatra, who helped Mike Myers (as Austin Powers) save the world from Dr. Evil.

Beyoncé had never expected to actually land the part. During the first few days of rehearsals, she was nearly overcome with nervousness. She told an interviewer from BeatBoxBetty.com:

"I didn't know what I was doing. I was just grateful to get the opportunity. I didn't think what would happen if it would go bad, I just did it and tried to do the best I could. I tried to learn. I felt like it was a new chapter of my life, a new way to grow as an artist."

When the movie was finally released, Beyoncé experienced another thrill that was as great as the first time she heard her voice on the radio—but this time she was seeing her face on a movie screen. She told the British Web site icnetwork.com:

"The premiere was the first time I saw the movie. It was really weird to see myself that big. But I was happy and relieved because I had been so nervous about it and I was like, Wow, that's really cool. I was proud."

Bad News

Despite Beyoncé's excitement with her new career opportunities, she was dismayed to learn that LeToya and LaTavia had filed another lawsuit, this time against Destiny's Child. This time around, they claimed that the lyrics from the single "Survivor" (from the album with the same name) violated a legal agreement that the group had made to never speak badly about each other.

Beyoncé didn't try to hide her hurt feelings. In her *Launch* interview, she said:

"It's really unfortunate that when you get successful, people try to steal your happiness. But they can't. . . . It's just sad. I don't want no drama, I don't want no enemies. All I want to do is go into the studio, write my music, do my movies, and perform. I'm not trying to hurt nobody, offend nobody. I'm just happy to be here, and it's just sad that all this other stuff comes along with it."

Faced with ongoing rumors and tension, Beyoncé kept pushing herself. By this time in her life, self-discipline and commitment to hard work were so ingrained in her that they were second nature for her.

Once her work for *Goldmember* was out of the way, she turned her attention back to her music career.

A lot of people questioned whether Beyoncé would be able to make it musically on her own, without backup from the rest of Destiny's Child. Beyoncé was about to prove she could.

Beyoncé's first feature-film role was as Foxxy Cleopatra in *Austin Powers in Goldmember*, starring Mike Myers. Together, Foxxy and Austin defeat the notorious Dr. Evil and save the world. There would be many more film roles to follow.

Singing Without Destiny's Child

Beyoncé's life was hectic, amazing, exciting. The excitement she had felt at performing on stage as a child had stayed with her. According to Internet Movie Database, she said:

> **"Every moment is not perfect. But it's definitely more good times than bad. You can't even compare. And when I'm on stage it feels incredible. There are certain nights that you know you hit that crazy note and you know that spin spinned extra fast. And you look out and people are just into it and you've worked so hard and now it's paying off and you can see why you dedicated your life to this."**

Beyoncé's voice earned her praise from around the world. In *Cove* magazine's countdown of the 100 Most Outstanding Pop Vocals of all time, she was placed at number seven (right behind Whitney Houston) and given a mark of forty-eight out of fifty for her impressive musical skills. Technically, her voice classified as a "dramatic mezzo-soprano," the sort of voice a classical opera singer might have. This meant she had an incredible range of more than three **octaves**.

Dangerously in Love

In May of 2003, Beyoncé's first solo single, "Crazy in Love," was released; it included a guest **rap** from Jay-Z, and it rapidly became one of the summer's biggest hits, staying for ten weeks at number one on *Billboard*'s Hot 100 Singles chart. Both the single and the album it came from, *Dangerously in Love*, sold more than two million copies by the end of the year.

In an interview with Yahoo! Music, Beyoncé described her first solo album:

> **"It's definitely a soulful, hard, hip-hop, gangster, ghetto, whatever-you-want-to-call-it album. It has a lot of soul, and it's very urban, and it's very fresh and new. . . . the untempo songs that are on the record are definitely club bangers that make you want to move."**

She told StarDose:

Beyoncé has experienced incredible success and rave reviews as a solo performer. She has performed in front of enthusiastic audiences, like this one in New York City in 2003, and won many awards for her individual efforts.

> **"I want [people] to hear all the musical influences, from hip-hop to rock to jazz. . . . Basically, this record was a chance for me to grow as a writer and a singer. . . . The experience was very liberating and therapeutic."**

Like the single, the album went to the top of the charts, both in the United Kingdom and Canada, as well as the United States, where it was at the top of both the pop and R&B charts. When the single and the album simultaneously topped the pop charts in both the United States and the United Kingdom, Beyoncé became the first to achieve this feat since Men at Work had done it in 1983. (The Beatles, Simon and Garfunkle, and Rod Stewart had pulled off the same accomplishment in the sixties and seventies.)

Toward the end of the summer, the album's second single, "Baby Boy," which featured **reggae** star Sean Paul, also began to climb the

"Crazy in Love" was a huge hit in the summer of 2003. The song also brought Beyoncé a new love—rap legend Jay-Z, who guest rapped on the track. In this photo from 2003, she and Jay-Z are seen performing at the Z-100 Jingle Ball.

charts. In the end, it too went on to become one of the year's biggest hits. Beyoncé released her third single from the album next. "Me, Myself, and I" also made *Billboard*'s Top 10.

In December of 2003, she learned she had been nominated for six Grammys (which was more than any other performer that year). And a couple of days after that, she received four *Billboard* awards, including New Female Artist of the Year and New R&B Artist of the Year.

During her *Billboard* acceptance speech, Beyoncé said:

> **"This is amazing! I want to first thank God for blessing me with all of these beautiful opportunities and wonderful people that I'm surrounded with. This has been an incredible year. I want to thank all my fans, and thank my sister Solange—I love you."**

The incredible year was one she would never forget. She told *Entertainment Weekly*, "It seems like every month something really huge happened." She starred in her second movie, *The Fighting Temptations*, opposite Cuba Gooding Jr., and she recorded a song for the movie with rappers Missy Elliott, Free, and MC Lyte. And *Entertainment Weekly* voted her one of its top-ten entertainers of 2003.

Controversy

But the amazing year had its difficult moments as well. Back in the summer, on the Fourth of July, Beyoncé was criticized by the Grant Memorial Association for her televised performance of "Crazy in Love" on the steps of Grant's Tomb. The association said she had danced in a "patently inappropriate" manner. President Grant's great-grandsons, Ulysses Grant Dietz and Chapman Foster, disagreed with the association, however. "The way the world is now, who cares?" said Foster. "Who knows? If the old guy were alive, he might have enjoyed it."

When she was a little girl, Beyoncé had seen herself as two people— "Sasha," the confident stage **persona**, and her off-stage, shy self. Now as an adult, she also separated her stage image from her "real-life" self. The Internet Movie Database quotes her as saying:

> **"Who I am on stage is very, very different to who I am in real life. But I don't see that having a sexy image when you are on stage means that you don't love God.**

No one knows what I'm really like from that. I like to walk around with bare feet and I don't like to comb my hair. I'm always so glammed up and so diva on stage and that's what they see. People don't understand that. . . . No one knows my personal relationship with God and it's not up to me to prove that to anyone. "

Beyoncé was a success worldwide. In this 2003 photo, she shows off MTV Europe music awards for Best Song and Best R&B Song. Beyoncé had a phenomenal 2003 and was looking forward to reuniting with Destiny's Child in 2004.

Going Strong

Ever since she was very young, Beyoncé had been pushing herself as hard as she could, and now that she was an adult, she showed no signs of letting up on herself. Despite how hard she was working, though, she said she didn't feel stressed about her life's pressures. She told an interviewer from Handbag.com:

> **"I love what I do. There are certain things that come along with it that I don't like, but it's a part of my job. Nobody's job is perfect. People are really critical in general and it's ten times worse when you're under a microscope, so it's hard to grow up under that. But I have people who love me, regardless of whether I sell another record or not."**

The strength she gained from her relationships was what kept Beyoncé strong. She maintained her close ties to her family (her cousin was her personal assistant, another cousin was her road manager, and her entire family visits her while she's on tour). Meanwhile, she also stayed close with the other members of Destiny's Child. As 2003 drew to a close, the group was planning to get back together again. They knew that wherever their careers took them, their friendship with each other would always last. "Beyoncé's still the same nine-year-old girl she was when I first knew her," Kelly Rowland told *Essence*.

And along with all the success 2003 had brought Beyoncé, it had also brought a new relationship into her life.

Relationships are important to Beyoncé, and she makes every effort to reach out and touch the lives of others. In 2003, love reached out and touched her in the form of rap legend Jay-Z. The couple is shown here at a fashion show in 2003.

5

Getting Personal

n the fall of 2002, Beyoncé was the featured vocalist on rapper Jay-Z's smash single, "03 Bonnie and Clyde." The following year, Beyoncé revealed that she and Jay-Z were dating. Jay-Z, one of the most popular and successful U.S. rappers of the late 1990s and early 2000s, is sometimes considered to be the best rapper alive.

Known for his blending of street and popular hip-hop, Jay-Z was one of the most respected rappers in the music industry before he announced his retirement from recording in 2004. He was later appointed the CEO of Def Jam Recordings. Clearly, Beyoncé had found her creative equal. The rumors circulated that the couple was engaged and planned to marry soon.

Beyoncé and Romance

It's hard for Beyoncé to expose her personal life to the world. Just as when she was younger, her performance self lived one life—and she kept her private life separate. She told Handbag.com, "I've always been a private person. . . . I'll tell my friends, but I just don't feel comfortable telling the whole world."

Beyoncé does admit that love is important to her—but she doesn't want to be defined by the man in her life. In an interview with *YM* magazine, she said: "I know girls who get boyfriends and then totally lose themselves. You can't do that, because the things that attracted him to you might get lost when you lose yourself." With that caution in mind, Beyoncé does hope one day to get married and have children. But she admits that falling in love takes courage. She told Yahoo! Music:

"There's definitely a dangerous feeling when you're in love, when it's real. And I think, for one, it's letting go and giving your heart to someone else and knowing that they have that control over your feelings. I know for me, who always tries to be so tough, that's the dangerous thing, that's the hard thing. But it's part of growing up and it's a part of life."

Living the life she has, Beyoncé realizes she made a lot of sacrifices growing up—and clearly, she doesn't intend to sacrifice her personal life forever. She told *Film Monthly*:

"When I'm able to, I want to do stuff that is fun. I've had the responsibility since I was 15 of someone who is 25 or 30, so now I have a lot of pressure. I make a lot of adult decisions, and that has forced me to grow up a little faster."

Friendships

Beyoncé remains close to the other girls in Destiny's Child. She told *Billboard* magazine at the time of their decision to split up, "Who knows what will happen in three, five, or ten years? The main thing is that we maintain our friendship and that we do it because we want to—not because it's a good business move."

After going their separate directions for three years, the girls reunited to create another album, *Destiny Fulfilled*, released in 2004. The album included the singles "Lose My Breath," "Soldier," and "Girl," all of which climbed to the top ten of the *Billboard* chart.

Destiny's Child went on tour together, but in Barcelona, Spain, in the summer of 2005, they shocked their fans by announcing from the stage that they planned to once again part company, at least professionally. Kelly Rowland made the announcement; she thanked their loyal fans and made sure everyone understood their decision did not mean the young women wouldn't continue to be friends. She said:

> **"After a lot of discussion and some deep soul-searching, we realized that our current tour has given us the opportunity to leave Destiny's Child on a high**

Even when they took time off from performing together, the members of Destiny's Child stayed close. Their relationship goes much deeper than the group. In 2004, the group reunited for *Destiny Fulfilled*. Here, Kelly, Beyoncé, and Michelle are shown at the 2005 Fashion Rocks event.

note, united in our friendship and filled with an over-whelming gratitude of our music, our fans, and each other. After all these wonderful years working together, we realized that now is the time to pursue our personal goals and solo efforts in earnest. This is a time of natural growth for all of us.**

Just a few months after they officially parted ways, though, the three members of Destiny's Child reunited in their hometown to sing the national anthem at the National Basketball Association's All-Star Game—but the trio insisted that the performance would be their last ever in Houston.

Family

Beyoncé has always been close to her family, and that hasn't changed as she's grown older. Her relationship with her mother is especially important to her. "Whatever I want," Beyoncé told BeatBoxBetty.com, "my mom is there for me." In an interview with Yahoo! Music, Beyoncé said:

"I feel blessed to know my mother, let alone to be her child. Just to be in her presence, I feel blessed, 'cause she is the definition of a phenomenal woman, and I want to be like her. . . . Every woman that's spent more than five minutes with her . . . loves her. She has that impact on everyone, and I just hope to be like that one day.

Beyoncé also speaks with pride of her father. When Yahoo! Music interviewed her, she described her dad as "a sincere person, a mature person, . . . a person who makes me laugh"; she admitted that these are the same qualities she wants in a man.

Beyoncé is especially close to her little sister, Solange. Solange has danced with Beyoncé at Destiny's Child concerts—and Solange has also proved that Beyoncé isn't the only Knowles with talent: Solange has released an album of her own. What's more, Solange has brought a new relationship into her big sister's life: Daniel Julez J. Smith, Solange's son and Beyoncé's nephew.

Beyoncé told Yahoo! Music: "I'm always so happy to see my parents and so happy to see my family, 'cause I'm always so homesick and they remind me of things that are real in life." In an interview with Cinema

Confidential, she explained: "My balance comes from my family. . . . They tell me when to calm down, take it down a couple notches. Then they tell me when I do something good."

Reaching Out to Others

Despite all the sacrifices her life demands, Beyoncé's life is a dream-come-true for her and her family—and now she is doing what she can to give back some of her good fortune to others. She sang a duet with Bono, "American Prayer," at a South African benefit to raise awareness of AIDS, and she has been involved with many other charities, including Katie Couric and the Entertainment Industry Foundation's *Queen*

Beyonce performs at charity events all over the world. In 2003, she joined U2's Bono for a duet at the 46664 concert in South Africa. Organized by former South Africa president Nelson Mandela, the concert raised awareness of the devastation of AIDS in Africa.

Destiny's Child also makes time to do good works. They visited Ronald McDonald Houses at stops on their Destiny Fulfilled . . . and Lovin' It tour. The group donated a portion of the tour's ticket sales to Ronald McDonald Charities.

Mary II benefit, the La Dolce Charity Concert, and a benefit for VH1 Save the Music.

A recently released Destiny's Child album, *Destiny's Child's #1's*, includes the song "Stand Up for Love," which was written for the 2005 World Children's Day; World Children's Day takes place every year on November 20 to raise awareness and funds for children's causes around the world. Beyoncé as well as Kelly and Michelle from Destiny's Child lent their voices and support as global ambassadors for the 2005 program. While they were on tour together, they visited Ronald McDonald Houses around the world. They also donated a portion of the North American ticket sales to Ronald McDonald Houses.

On September 16, 2005, Beyoncé participated in the Fashion for Relief show in New York City, a benefit for AmeriCares to help those whose lives were disrupted by Hurricane Katrina. (Nicole Richie, Irina Pantaeva, Wyclef Jean, Naomi Campbell, and Kelly Osborne were some of the other stars who also participated in the fashion show.)

Earlier, Beyoncé and Kelly Rowland, along with Beyoncé's mom, dad, and sister, founded the Knowles-Rowland Center for Youth, a community outreach center in downtown Houston. After Hurricane Katrina, the family extended their center's mission and formed the Survivor Foundation. The foundation will provide **transitional** housing for storm **evacuees** in the Houston area.

Making Movies

Beyoncé is still pursuing her acting career as well. She was selected for the starring role of Xania in the *Pink Panther*, which was released early in 2006. Steve Martin played opposite her as Inspector Clouseau.

In 2005, Beyoncé continued her acting career as Xania in the film *Pink Panther*, starring French actor Jean Reno and American funnyman Steve Martin. Her fans eagerly anticipated her performance in *Dreamgirls*, the long-awaited film version of the Broadway smash hit.

Beyoncé plans to pursue her acting career in the years to come. She had always dreamed of having a role in a musical one day, the sort of movie that would showcase her singing and dancing talents as well as her acting. Her role in *Dreamgirls*, the movie version of the Broadway hit, gave her that opportunity.

Whether as part of Destiny's Child or as a solo artist, as an actress, businessperson, or fashion icon, life and the future looks good for Beyoncé Knowles. She's worked hard, but she knows that she's been lucky, too.

Facing the Future

Despite the stress her life has put on her, Beyoncé doesn't feel that success has changed her. She told the interviewer from *Film Monthly*: "I still like roller coasters, talking on the phone, and being silly. I like when people are silly because then I can be silly too." And in the end, she wouldn't change her life. "I love what I do," she said, "and I love to perform; that's what fuels me."

When the interviewer from Yahoo! Music asked her where she saw herself in another ten years, she replied: "Hopefully, I'll be settled down, starting a family. . . . I just want to be happy. I want Destiny's Child to be friends and I want to be making my mark in history."

Beyoncé would like to do something that involves teaching and children one day. She might even want to teach art. (Painting is one of her private emotional outlets, one that she never shows anyone.) She believes that creativity is good for kids, that it helps keep them out of trouble and builds their self-esteem. She told Yahoo! Music: "I love teaching, and I think that I'm a natural-born leader and teaching is so fun for me, so I would like to teach something creative so kids have a place to escape."

As a little girl, Beyoncé dreamed that one day her creativity would lead her all the way to the top. Now that her dream has become a reality, she admits that there are some aspects of her life she didn't expect when she was a child. She told BeatBoxBetty.com:

"You don't dream about certain things—like people hiding under blankets taking pictures of you—but it's everything and more. It's more beautiful than you could ever imagine but it's also harder than you ever imagined. Like everything in life, there are sacrifices—but it's worth it."

1981 Beyoncé Giselle Knowles is born in Houston, Texas, on September 4.

1992 Appears on *Star Search* as part of the group Girls Tyme.

1995 Destiny's Child signs its first record contract.

1997 Destiny's Child signs with Columbia Records.

1998 Destiny's Child releases its first album, *Destiny's Child.*

Destiny's Child wins three awards at Soul Train Lady of Soul Awards.

Whitney Houston invites Destiny's Child to her birthday party.

1999 The album *The Writing's on the Wall* is released.

2000 LaTavia Roberson and LeToya Luckett leave Destiny's Child and are replaced by Michelle Williams and Farrah Franklin; Franklin quits five months later.

2001 The album *Survivor* is released and debuts at number one.

Beyoncé wins Songwriter of the Year Award at the ASCAP Pop Music Awards.

Destiny's Child wins two Grammy Awards.

Destiny's Child wins five *Billboard* awards.

2002 Beyoncé appears as Foxxy Cleopatra in *Austin Powers in Goldmember.*

Destiny's Child wins one Grammy Award.

2003 Beyoncé becomes the first artist to have the number-one single and album on the pop charts in both the United States and the United Kingdom.

Beyoncé begins dating Jay-Z.

Beyoncé's first single, "Crazy in Love" and album, *Dangerously in Love* are released.

Entertainment Weekly names Beyoncé one of its top-ten entertainers of the year.

Beyoncé remakes "The Closer I Get to You" with Luther Vandross.

Beyoncé stars in *The Fighting Temptations.*

In a controversial production, Beyoncé performs "Crazy in Love" on the steps of Grant's Tomb.

Destiny's Child receives four *Billboard* awards.

2004 Destiny's Child releases *Destiny Fulfilled*.

Beyoncé wins five Grammy Awards, tying the record for most Grammys won by a female artist, previously held by Alicia Keys, Norah Jones, and Lauryn Hill.

2005 Beyoncé and her mother begin a clothing line.

Destiny's Child announces they are breaking up.

Destiny's Child performs at Live 8 Benefit concert.

2006 Beyoncé is nominated for a Grammy Award; Destiny's Child is nominated for two Grammy Awards.

Destiny's Child sings the national anthem at the NBA All-Star Game in Houston, Texas.

Beyoncé stars in *The Pink Panther* and *Dreamgirls*.

Beyoncé receives four NAACP Award nominations for both her music and her acting.

Beyoncé receives two Golden Globe nominations for *Dreamgirls*: Best Actress-Motion Picture, Musical, or Comedy and Best Original Song for "Listen."

Discography
Solo Albums
2003   *Dangerously in Love*

2004   *Maximum Beyoncé*
        Live at Wembley

2006   *B'Day*

Number-one Singles
2003   "Baby Boy" (with Sean Paul)
        "Crazy in Love"

2006   "Check on It" (with Slim Thug)
        "Déjà vu"

Book
2002   Knowles, Beyoncé, Kelly Rowland, and Michelle Williams. *Soul Survivors: The Official Biography of Destiny's Child.* New York: Regan Books, 2002.

Selected Television Appearances
2002   *Saturday Night Live*

2003   *AFI Life Achievement Award: A Tribute to Robert DeNiro*; *The Barbara Walters Special: The 10 Most Fascinating People of 2003*; *Punk'd*; *V. Graham Norton*; *VH1 Divas Duet*; *Macy's 4th of July Spectacular*; *Boogie*; *The Tonight Show with Jay Leno*; *The Oprah Winfrey Show*

2004   *Fade to Black*; *Fashion Rocks*; *Maxim Hot 100*; *Michael Jackson: The One*; *The Wayne Brady Show*; *The Oprah Winfrey Show*

2005   *ESPY Awards*; *The Kennedy Center Honors: A Celebration of the Performing Arts*; *Live 8*; *Rockin' the Corps: An American Thank You*; *The Oprah Winfrey Show*

2006   *Top of the Pops*; *Late Show with David Letterman*

Film
2001   *Carmen: A Hip Hopera*

2002   *Austin Powers in Goldmember*

2003   *The Fighting Temptations*

2006   *Dreamgirls*
        The Pink Panther

Video

2002 *The World of Austin Powers*

2003 *Beyoncé: Unauthorized*

2004 *Beyoncé: Live at Wembley*

Awards

2000 Grammy Award: Best R&B Song (writer, "Say My Name")

2002 ASCAP Awards: Most Performed Songs

2003 MTV Europe Awards: Best R&B Award and Best Song of the Year

MTV Video Music Awards: Best Choreography in a Video; Best R&B Video; Best Female Video—Winner 20th MTV Video Music Awards

Grammy Awards: Best Rap/Sung Collaboration ("Crazy in Love," with Jay-Z), Best Contemporary R&B Album (*Beyoncé*), Best R&B Song (writer, "Crazy in Love," with Jay-Z and Rich Harrison), Best R&B Performance by a Duo or Group with Vocals ("The Closer I Get," with Luther Vandross), Best Female R&B Vocal Performance ("Dangerously in Love 2")

2004 Black Entertainment Awards: Best Female R&B Artist winner

Brit Award: International Female Solo Artist of the Year

Black Reel Award: Best Song

Grammy Awards: Best R&B Song for "Crazy in Love" featuring Jay-Z; Best Rap/Sung Collaboration for "Crazy in Love" featuring Jay-Z; Best Contemporary R&B Album for Dangerously In Love; Best R&B Vocal Performance—Female; Best R&B Vocal Performance by a Duo or Group for "The Closer I Get To You" (with Luther Vandross)

MTV Video Music Awards: Female Video of the Year

NAACP Image Award: Entertainer of the Year

Sammy Davis Jr. Award: Entertainer of the Year—Female

Soul Train Music Awards: Best Female RB/Soul Album

2005 Grammy Award: Best R&B Performance by a Duo or Group with Vocals ("So Amazing," with Stevie Wonder)

2006 Grammy Award: Best Contemporary R&B Album (*B'day*)

Books

Gittins, Ian. *Destiny's Child.* London: Carlton Books, 2002.

Kenyatta, Kelly. *Destiny's Child.* Hollywood, Calif.: Busta Books, 2001.

Knowles, Beyoncé, Kelly Rowland, and Michelle Williams. *Soul Survivors: The Official Biography of Destiny's Child.* New York: Regan Books, 2002.

Knowles, Tina. *Destiny's Style.* New York: Regan Books, 2002.

Rodway, Keith. *Destiny's Child: The Unauthorized Biography in Words and Pictures.* London: Chrome Dreams, 2001.

Tracy, Kathleen. *Beyoncé.* Hockessin, Del.: Mitchell Lane, 2005.

Magazines

Bagley, Christopher. "Above and Beyonce." *W*, May 1, 2002.

Greenberg, Julee. "Beyonce Talks Fashion." *WWD*, May 12, 2004.

Mayo, Kierna. "The Power of Three." *CosmoGirl!*, March 1, 2005.

Norment, Lynn. "Beyonce Heats Up Hollywood." *Ebony*, July 1, 2002.

Web Sites

Beyoncé Knowles
www.beyonce-knowles.com

Beyoncé Knowles
www.1greatcelebsite.com/beyonce_knowles/interview.htm

Official Beyoncé Knowles Fan Club
www.beyonceonline.com

civil rights demonstrations—protests on behalf of the rights that all citizens of a society are supposed to have.

debuted—made its first appearance.

diva—an extremely arrogant or temperamental woman.

evacuees—people who are removed from a place of danger and sent somewhere safer.

favoritism—the practice of giving special treatment or unfair advantages to a person.

inaugurated—dedicated ceremoniously.

octaves—in music, eight-note intervals.

persona—the image that somebody shows the outside world.

R&B—rhythm and blues; a blending of jazz and blues.

rap—popular music style characterized by spoken rhyming vocals and often featuring a looped electronic beat in the background.

reggae—popular music, originally from Jamaica, that combines elements of rock, calypso, and soul.

tableau—a visually dramatic scene.

transitional—relating to a change from one state or condition to another.

Aguilera, Christina, 21, 28, 29
AIDS, 51
American Idol, 20
American Music Awards, 15
American Society of Composers, Authors, and Publishers Pop Music Awards, 35
AmeriCares, 52–53
Amerie, 16
ASCAP, 34
Austin Powers in Goldmember, 37, 39

Barbara Davis Center for Childhood Diabetes, 13
Beatles, the, 41
Berry, Halle, 14
BET Awards, 12
Billboard Awards, 35, 40, 43, 48
Black, Clint, 12
Bono, 51

Campbell, Naomi, 53
Carousel of Hope, 13, 14
CFDA Fashion Awards, 21
Charlie's Angels, 35
civil rights demonstrations, 19
Clapton, Eric, 12
Cleopatra, Foxxy, 37, 39
Cliché, 23
Columbia Records, 29
Cove magazine, 40

Def Jam Recordings, 47
depression, 32
Destiny Fulfilled . . . and Lovin' It Tour, 14, 16
Destiny's Child, 14–16, 18, 22, 27, 28, 29–36, 37, 38, 40, 44, 45, 48, 49, 40, 52, 54

Dolls, The, 23
Dreamgirls, 17, 53, 54

Elliott, Missy, 10, 43
Entertainment Industry Foundation's *Queen Mary II* benefit, 51–52
Europe music awards, 44

Fighting Temptations, The, 43
Flack, Roberta, 17
46664 concert, 51
fragrance, 14
Franklin, Farrah, 32, 33
Free, 43

Girls Tyme, 20
Gooding, Jr., Cuba, 43
Grammy Awards, 9, 10, 15, 17, 22, 31, 34, 35, 43
Grant's Tomb performance, 43
Groban, Josh, 14

Hathaway, Donny, 17
Hill, Faith, 14
Hill, Lauryn, 9
House of Dereon, 11, 12, 15, 16
Houston, Whitney, 30, 31, 40
Hurricane Katrina, 53

Jay-Z, 40, 42, 46, 47
Jean, Wyclef, 53
Jones, Norah, 9
Jones, Tommy Lee, 29

Keys, Alicia, 9, 10
Knowles, Mathew (father), 18, 19, 20, 22, 23, 27, 29, 32, 50, 53
Knowles, Solange (sister), 26, 27, 30, 50, 53
Knowles, Tina (mother), 11, 12, 18, 19, 20, 21, 23, 27, 50, 53